THE HUMAN CONNECTION

THE HUMAN CONNECTION

PHOTOGRAPHS & STORIES FROM BANGLADESH & NEPAL

Jeremy Fokkens

RMB

CONTENTS

INTRODUCTION

As I stepped off the plane onto the pot-hole-riddled tarmac, my first thought was "holy *shit* it's hot here!" The date was April 21, 2011, and I had just spent the past thirty hours on three different airplanes before arriving in Kathmandu, Nepal. You always have preconceived notions of what the climate of a country should be, no matter how much research you do, and it is never quite what you expect. Once my naive anticipation of snow had cleared and my body was slowly adjusting to my now sweat-drenched shirt, I lumbered out of the terminal building, one pack slung across my chest, the other on my back.

I quickly found a taxi away from all the other locals and travellers that were being politely accosted by the hundred or so eager cabbies looking to score an overpriced fare. Unfortunately I felt sorry for my driver, as he knew right away after sizing me up and giving me a price on my destination that I was not going to budge like all the other virgin travellers that were still being paraded around like cattle behind me. Once in the taxi I rolled down the window and gazed out peacefully on the chaos of Kathmandu. The car looked similar to a Chevy Chevette, just without seat belts and with a hole in its floor where I could see the road passing underneath me. This is the part of travelling I enjoy the most: taking in all the smells, imperfections, noise, congestion and unfamiliarity of the people and their environment. I never knew I missed Asia so much until that moment.

My plans for this trip started when I had returned from a jaunt to southeast Asia in 2008. It was during that odyssey that I started to get a clearer understanding of what I wanted to say as a photographer, as I aimlessly walked streets in Vietnam, Cambodia and Laos for three months. So when I decided to go to South Asia I used the same approach: just dive in head first without really checking to see how deep the water is. (Oddly enough, that's exactly how I almost drowned when I was five years old, on my first trip to Australia.) I immediately started researching countries and regions where travellers were not visiting, including places rarely, if ever, covered in mainstream media. I prefer going to places I have little or no familiarity with. It forces me to be vulnerable, yet this feeling of the unknown is what takes me out of my comfort zone and into my element where I can communicate and connect with my photographic subjects.

The plan was to travel to Nepal, Bangladesh and India for no set amount of time, camera in hand every step of the way, volunteering for grassroots and local initiatives when I could, and all under one mission, which was to take pictures and build a body of work I could be proud of. So, with a one-way ticket to Kathmandu, forty pounds of camera gear and one change of clothes, I put my business on hold and promised myself a trip where I could focus on nothing but photography. One thing I had not planned on getting from this trip turned out to be something greater than just taking pictures: finding a voice where photography would be my means of inspiring and telling stories of people from all walks of life.

Depending on how you travel there and your reasons for visiting, Nepal is a place that will nourish your soul. Through the generosity of its people, a warm, heartfelt smile will be a daily encounter that often will happen several times in the span of walking two city blocks. From enjoyment of simple things such as sitting in a food stall gorging on the local cuisine of dhal, momos and chai to venturing out into the country's vast landscape of the world's tallest peaks, Nepal will challenge you and push you to your very limits. This is always the joy of travelling, as it puts everything in perspective. It humbles you and you discover things about yourself. I never knew what a simple life meant and I never knew what travel meant until I started pursuing experiences with less comfort, away from the familiar, seeking both physical and mental adventure.

Before I made my first leap into the world of documentary photography in 2008, I had these crazy ideas and situations that I would constantly unfurl in my own head, picturing myself always on the move by helicopter or jeep, photographing a thousand different stories, running into a mob of angry protesters, hanging by one hand off the side of a mountain while dramatically taking pictures with the other hand like some sort of action hero. These thoughts blinded me from really seeing the reason why I travel now and why I am a photographer. The best advice on this I ever heard came from a close friend, who is also an artist: "Don't force it." Three simple words that have stuck with me ever since I took the leap into photographing people in foreign countries and at home in Canada. You cannot force creativity. It is a process that comes from pursuing knowledge, engaging in a community, failing miserably, being open to new places and environments and embracing more failures than successes.

The act of just physically moving around Nepal was an adventure all on its own and one that many travellers who visit the country could write several books about, I'm sure. One of my more memorable experiences was meeting a local pilot in the town of Surkhet, where I was volunteering for a local orphanage. "James" was from New Zealand and we went out one evening and had one too many beers. Some time later, James informally but generously offered to fly me into the Humla district, in the far northwest of Nepal, by labelling me as cargo on his manifest. The morning of the scheduled departure I found myself sitting among 50-kilo bags of rice and a host of other food supplies and medical equipment bound for the small village of Simikot. Once we were in the air and reaching our cruising altitude, James motioned for me to come forward to the flightdeck. I thought I was going to just briefly ogle the view, but the first officer unbuckled her seatbelt and invited me to take her place.

Now, I have flown in many planes before, even as a teenager. My best friend, Ryan, was a pilot at 16, so when all our friends were getting their first cars, Ryan and I were off in little Cessnas doing flybys over farmers' fields, our parents' houses, even over highways, with barely 100 feet between us and the ground. But here, over craggy Nepal, the view was breathtaking and James even let me take the controls for 20 minutes. I have flown over the Canadian Rockies many times in aircraft of all shapes and sizes, but there is something different about the Himalaya. It's wild, it's daunting and it makes you feel very insignificant and helpless.

After about 45 minutes of flying we could see the gravel runway and the little village of Simikot, situated atop a small plateau with nothing but massive snow-capped mountains surrounding it. The landing was far from smooth and once the plane taxied to a neutral area, I was greeted by a man named Santos, whom James knew quite well. James had given Santos a heads-up about my arrival, to make sure I would have a place to stay in Simikot. As we set off toward the guest house I was in shock at the views that surrounded this tiny town. At 2900 metres above sea level the air was cool and the sun's intensity was noticeably stronger. I could feel it penetrating my fragile skin with only minutes of exposure. A perfect bluebird sky contrasted with snow-covered mountain-tops. Santos led me to my room, which consisted of two beds and a table. The bathroom was outside, in a separate shack adjacent to the guesthouse, with a communal sink and a solar-powered hot shower. After pausing to absorb the view, I decided to stroll around the town to clear my head, get my bearings, meet some of the locals and just take everything in. I was shocked at how remote this place was, with little huts and other villages you could see in the valleys rising up like staircases thousands of metres above the valley floor. There are no roads to Simikot; the only way you can get here is by plane unless you want to walk 10 days from the nearest road. The locals still use yaks and donkeys to bring in supplies from neighbouring regions like China. They've only recently added the airport – more like a dirt track with a shack beside it – to enable more frequent trips and deliver more goods, if only during the summer. Come fall, all flights cease due to the unpredictable weather and heavy snow during the winter.

My two weeks in Simikot was a real eye-opener as to the type of people that inhabit the area. I spent my days exploring the town and surrounding villages, getting to know local people. When I was away from Simikot, I slept in a one-man tent, photography gear and all. People let me sleep on top of their massive homes, which were twenty feet high and made completely of brick and mud. These houses were surprisingly cool even when daytime temperatures reached into the mid-thirties. It rained almost every night, with winds that made me wonder if I was going to be blown right off the roof. Some nights were better than others. Some were terrible, especially the night I discovered a hole in my tent, which forced me to sleep with my photo gear between my legs.

Thehe was one of the small places nearby that I visited often. The village is perched on an outcrop of a mountain with sheer drops of more than thirty metres as you approach. People live in mud huts that are all joined together, resembling a jumble of stairs sticking out from the mountainside. If you were to kick a soccer ball off the top, it would drop hundreds of metres, bouncing off the odd roof on its way down and finally plunging off a cliff. It was a very poor town, with clear signs that it lacked basic necessities such as healthcare, education, nutrition, even running water in some places. The good news, though, is that I met up with a grassroots foundation that was working with the locals to fix those issues, including programs that supported horticulture, biogas and irrigation.

When photographing in any country, I try to stick to some sort of schedule and take maximum advantage of morning and evening light. In Kathmandu I had a guide for about a third of my time there, which happened by sheer luck. And of course, there's a back story to that.

You see, before I became a photographer I had been a professional dancer. And on this trip to Nepal, after countless hours photographing in extreme heat and less than glamorous conditions for weeks on end, I was starting to need a little break, so I figured why not see if there was a dance studio in Kathmandu. And after a short Internet search, it turned out there was! It was a salsa studio owned by an ex-Montrealer named Katia. So of course I gave this person a call. I told Katia what I was doing in the country and asked if she could use a dance teacher. As it happened, she could, and she would put me up for six weeks if I taught two or three times a week at her studio. I had never taught a dance class in a foreign country before, especially one where Nepali teenagers and adults were learning hip hop solely from watching videos on YouTube, mimicking moves and styles from pop stars like Michael Jackson and Justin Timberlake. It was great to give Katia's students a bit of a foundation in just basic movement and then work our way up into more stylized forms of dance. My classes would number upwards of forty students and they loved every minute of it. They soaked up every ounce of dance knowledge they could and would return week after week to show me how well they had practised last week's moves.

Anyway, it was through teaching at the dance studio that I met Ashok, a local salsa teacher. I asked him if he would be willing to take me around Kathmandu three or four times a week on his days off when he was not studying or teaching. We settled on a fair wage, and for the remainder of my time in Nepal I had my own personal guide. Ashok would take me wherever I wanted, all over the Kathmandu Valley, on the back of his 75 cc moped. He would also translate

so I could talk with locals, giving me a true Nepali experience.

It is sometimes hard to adjust in a place where the people, the culture, the society, even government policies, sometimes hinder your plans and expectations of a country where its own citizens are scratching their heads right along with you. No one can give you a valid reason or even understand why themselves; in Nepal, as with so many other places in this world, you just have to accept it. But without setbacks, bad days, great days, even days when you get litres of street juice splashed all over you and your expensive gear, we could not create those special connections that come from the sheer love of the craft. Photographers take pride in what they do and will go to almost any lengths to continue taking good pictures, even great ones. We cannot grow individually without these experiences, and from there we cannot move forward. In three incredible months in Nepal I had the honour of meeting so many fantastic and beautiful people from such a vast variety of countries, including Ireland, Germany, the USA, Belgium, Canada, the Netherlands, Spain and of course the Nepalis themselves. The people of Nepal are by far some of the most generous and warm-hearted individuals I have ever come across in all my travels. Their carefree spirits and their constant drive to satisfy even the simplest request make you feel as if you are an extension of their very own family.

THE BRICKYARDS OF SURKHET

I made a conscious effort to get up extra early one day because I had discovered this amazing brickmaking factory the day before. I was in the town of Surkhet volunteering for a local orphanage (run by the Blinknow Foundation) that also educates some 350 students, and before I made my way to the school that day, I wanted to spend a few hours photographing this place just for the shock factor and to satisfy my curiosity.

So, I awoke at 5 a.m., gathered up my gear and headed toward the centre of town, veering off the main road next to the side of a small bridge. I continued to walk, kicking up dust, given it was already well into the dry season, past riverbank communities whose shacks looked a little damaged from a storm a couple of days before. I crossed numerous rice paddies, yielded the right of way to a herd of goats and water buffalo and finally arrived at my destination. I was approaching a clearing where you could see a dozen or so people slowly carrying what looked like large boxes on their backs. As I got closer I realized they were carrying stacks of bricks using tumplines: ropes looped from a pad on their forehead down their back and under the load. I spent that day introducing myself, making a variety of hand gestures to establish communication and adding the occasional drawing on a notepad I carry wherever I go. The locals working the brickyards of Surkhet were very welcoming, letting me go wherever I wanted, and they were very willing and curious to have their photo taken. By 10 o'clock the temperature had already soared to a stifling 35°C, which can be pretty uncomfortable all by itself, let alone all the dust, chemicals and debris in the air.

Brickyards in Nepal vary in size depending on where you are in the country. Some are large-scale industrial operations, but many, as at Surkhet, are essentially artisanal, using a basic technology called a "bull trench kiln." These brick-curing ovens are quite simple: a large rectangular hole in the ground about two metres deep. Workers harvest wet clay from the earth and hand-shape it into bricks using moulds that resemble cookie cutters. They leave the clay bricks to dry in the sun awhile, then arrange them in the pit, leaving a small space between each one so that the heat will bake all the bricks evenly. The "green" bricks are then covered with fine sand and ash and the kiln is fuelled on top of the pit, usually with coal, occasionally with firewood. The heat draws any remaining moisture out of the clay and causes the bricks to harden.

The brickyards I visited in both Nepal and Bangladesh employed anywhere from 10 people all the way up to hundreds, ranging in age from 12 to 80. It was quite upsetting to see children working in such conditions, especially with thousands of bricks stacked unstably high with only narrow passages in between, plus the abundance of chemicals and fine debris that the workers inhale daily. This got me asking questions as to why this type of labour exists. Is it because there was a need for more bricks due to the booming economy in Nepal at that time? Perhaps health and safety regulations are not on the agenda for the companies that run these outfits where labourers work in fear of losing their job if they speak out. Quite possibly it could be lack of education about the materials they work with, not knowing what health problems could arise due to exposure.

Pashupatinath is a holy place boasting Hindu temples, public altars, shrines and old architecture. It is situated on both sides of the sacred Bagmati River in the eastern part of Kathmandu. Most people who travel to Nepal usually come here to get a glimpse of the temples, visit the majestic Himalayas and do a little shopping for paraphernalia in the local street stands.

Locals and tourists alike flock to this place to witness Kathmandu's residents paying their respects to loved ones who have passed away. In Nepal people do not bury their dead; they cremate the remains at sites along the banks of the Bagmati. These sites are outdoors and completely open to the public, so anyone may view the proceedings of what westerners would call a funeral. The dead are put on steel-beam structures along the river to hold the remains in place. Wood is placed under the body as well as on top, and after religious rites are performed, the remains are burned until there is nothing left but ash. Another sign that someone has passed away is that occasionally you will see Nepali men with their heads shaven clean, leaving nothing but a little lock of hair on the back.

We all know death is a part of life but I find it very refreshing how willingly and widely death is accepted here and in other Asian countries. People in Nepal die every day in homes, streets, villages and hospitals and from curable or controllable diseases such as flu, diarrhea, tuberculosis, waterborne viruses and infections. Fatal road accidents are a daily occurrence, the fourth-greatest cause of death in Nepal. Death is an everyday event everywhere in the world, of course, but I think most people in Nepal have seen death first-hand at least once, and it seems to facilitate their carefree acceptance of the inevitable fate of every living thing on this planet. In Canada, on the other hand, I think the majority of people are afraid of dying or even thinking about it. It has become a complete taboo. But you can't blame people for being scared. Heck, it still makes me a little nervous. It is the unknown. Is there a white light or will it only be lights out? We just don't know. But rather than run away from the inevitable, why not try and understand what is so frightening and see how we can learn from other cultures to accept and celebrate death as much as we celebrate birth?

When I first heard of Pashupatinath from other travellers, I actually had no interest in the temples and monasteries, never mind the entrance fees and the cheap memorabilia you are pressured to purchase from every man, woman or child you make eye contact with. Rather, my reason for coming to this holy place was to visit a specific ashram not frequented by tourists or even many locals. It was also to volunteer for a special cause that involved Nepali seniors who have been abandoned by their families, whether because the families could no longer support them or they were a disgrace because of old age or disabilities.

As you enter the grounds of Pashupatinath, there is a large, square, weathered brown building immediately to your right as you approach the admission gates of the several main temples that are visited by tourists. This structure looks a little out of character compared to the rest of the buildings on the Pashupatinath grounds because it doesn't even have a gate, let alone a Nepali attendant collecting your admission fee. As you approach the ashram you go down stone and concrete steps that descend a couple of metres below ground level. As you near the entrance, you start to hear sounds of music and voices where a set of wooden steps covered by an archway marks the entrance to the ashram. As I made my way up the steps and under the archway, I was suddenly greeted by an array of beautiful faces chanting and singing, accompanied by a single drummer and a harmonium player, while a hint of sweet incense gently lingered in the air. The people creating this colourful music and celebration were residents of the ashram, who greeted me with an abundance of head nods, clasped hands and namastes.

The outer structure of the ashram has two levels, with an open courtyard in the centre. The two indoor levels are living quarters for the residents who were so warmly welcoming me. The centre courtyard contains five major, structured altars where residents and locals perform their daily religious rites and offerings. As you walk around the centre temple you come to a door directly opposite where you entered. As I walked through this second entrance, my senses were suddenly overtaken by a smell I can only describe as … death. But please do not take that word in a negative sense, as the word "death" should not have a negative stigma attached to it, which is one of the reasons for the series of images beginning at page 85.

This separate area connected to the main ashram has another, smaller, L-shaped structure where about 20 elderly residents are cared for by local and international volunteers, including Sisters of Mother Theresa (Missionaries of Charity). These residents are extremely aged and suffer from blindness, dementia, Down syndrome or amputation and are here to live out the rest of their natural life. I was brought here by a woman named Fanny Vandewiele, who had been volunteering here for the past two years. As Fanny introduces me to everyone I suddenly get this warm feeling because of the palpable joy in many of these seniors and how similar they are to small children. As I walk around taking in all the faces I notice men and women fighting with one another over a juice box. I see a man with Down syndrome constantly poking and harmlessly annoying some of the women for his own satisfaction. I see people napping, people laughing, people grunting. I see people sitting quietly, saying a few words to each other every so often. I can't help but think we leave this world the same way we are born into it, and honestly it's quite beautiful and comforting to see.

The facility has working toilets, running water with solar panels for hot water, beds, blankets, clothing and food, all your basic necessities. But it was not always so. When Fanny first came here to volunteer she noticed that the place was almost, for lack of a better word, uninhabitable. The Nepali government had built this facility many years ago to provide an adequate place for the aged to live out their lives. More recently a Dutch philanthropist had donated a substantial amount of money to rebuild the ashram because of a lack of maintenance that was never addressed by the Pashupatinath Trust, which was responsible for all the necessary upkeep. Unfortunately, like many Nepal organizations, governments and NGOs, this one too was corrupt, greedy and lazy. The ashram was never maintained again, even after this sizeable donation, and the people there continued to suffer greatly. One day as Fanny and the MC Sisters were working, water suddenly started pouring in through the roof and the seniors were literally sleeping in the rain.

That's when Fanny Vandewiele had had enough and decided to do something. She gained the confidence of the MC Sisters and four Nepali volunteers – Manish Joshi, Riti Pyakurel, Sudharsan Pradhan and Maya (whose last name I unfortunately was not able to get) – and together they pooled their contacts, skills and resources to start a complete reconstruction of this facility behind the main ashram. Fanny even managed to help fund the project from her own pocket as well as organizing fundraisers in her home country of Belgium to cover all costs. But raising the money wasn't the half of it. They also faced a slew of obstacles along the way, including strikes, building code changes stemming from bureaucratic obstacles, threats, and locals saying they would help but failing to ever show up. To add insult to injury, the monsoon season was right around the corner. Nevertheless, Fanny's team and the MC Sisters got it done, all with their own hands. They had rebuilt the living quarters, installed a brand new roof with not a single leak, purchased a solar panel heating system for the water tanks, built proper washrooms and overall made a much more pleasant environment for the aged residents of Pashupatinath.

I spent three weeks there on and off, volunteering at what Fanny likes to call "a little piece of heaven."

BANGLADESH

When I arrived in Dhaka, Bangladesh, I was shocked at how nice the airport was, given the country's reputation as the slum of all Asia as I'd heard when travelling in southeast Asia and Nepal. As I collected my bags and made my way outside to hail a cab I was immediately hit with what felt like a brick wall of humidity. I am not exaggerating when I say it's comparable to opening a preheated oven at 500 degrees. During the monsoon season, temperature and humidity soar to a point where excessive sweating could become the latest fad. When the "winter" months arrive, the climate calms down to a more moderate 25°C, with evening temperatures around 15°.

With a bit of trouble finding a place to stay, due to my cab driver not being able to understand my very broken Bengali, I managed to finally get my bearings to settle in for the night at a very dodgy hotel, which I later learned was frequented by men looking for a

good time. And did I mention waking up at 1 a.m. to find myself covered in bedbug bites? The next day, I headed out bright and early to do a little exploring and hit up the markets to get the necessary supplies to make life a little easier in a new country. Realizing that everyone here has a cellphone and that owning one makes things so much more convenient, I immediately bought a new SIM card. I also acquired an up-to-date city map and immediately located the fresh fruit stands and a café with Internet access.

The one thing that shocked me about this country, given its reputation, was the hospitality. Bangladeshis are the most welcoming people I have ever met in any country. Anyone and everyone will help you. In my first two weeks I had complete strangers offer me a place to stay in their homes and invite me to dinners and other functions. I was even invited on a family vacation to northern parts of the country. Bangladeshis live to please guests, foreigners and friends of friends. The people here do not possess much, but their heart and generosity make up for every negative experience I encountered.

After getting in contact with a variety of NGO people, students, writers, journalists and random expatriates, I started feeling a bit overwhelmed by the mega-city of Dhaka, so I decided to explore more of the country by first heading south and starting to work on a photo series about fishermen.

Bangladesh is without a doubt the most extreme of all the counties I have visited so far – in everything, both good and bad. There are millions of people; drivers are crazier; there is food everywhere, delicious and spicy. But poverty is also very prevalent and in plain sight. People stare at you constantly, though seemingly only if you're a foreigner or you're arguing with a local in the middle of the street. Everybody sings, everybody dances, everybody has a cellphone, sometimes two

or three. There are more tea stalls than we have Starbucks on every corner. People spit as much as they breathe in a day, and the weather is intense. Bangladesh is a place where you catch a child trying to steal your wallet and an hour later thief and victim have become best friends... this actually happened to me. The smiles here are endless and this is one of those places that everyone needs to experience.

Life here is extremely difficult for most residents, both in the big cities and in the country. A Bangladeshi told me that the unemployment rate has reached 40 per cent, making it extremely hard for everyone, educated or not, to find a job to support themselves and their families, especially when the majority of households have only one breadwinner, usually the man/husband.

Bangladesh gave me a roller coaster of emotions and opportunities, and it pushed me to my very limits both physically and mentally. I travelled and lived there for five months, and in my final two weeks it was extremely difficult to find any motivation to actually pick up my camera. I started to become very moody; even the smallest thing would aggravate me. I was starting to burn out. It was hindering my relationships with subjects and stories, and all this negative energy was starting to show in my photographs. There is always a need for improvement, where you push yourself to go harder, longer, and never stop searching and shooting. I am a perfectionist, but only human. Unfortunately we are not built like robots to function 24/7. Sometimes I had to force myself to just step back, relax, have a cold beer, put the camera down and get away from it all.

Across Airport Road lies one of the rail lines that runs through Dhaka, where one of my previous excursions had taken me onto the roof of a train. That little stunt gave me a quick tour through the city and showed me some very intriguing and interesting places. So I decided it would be a good idea to walk that same rail line to see what images I could capture.

This particular day turned out to be an interesting one where subconsciously I was photographing children the entire day. Occasionally I would photograph an adult, but for every grownup I had about 40 children pictured. It was a very playful day filled with laughs, children climbing all over me, showing them the proper way to give high fives, which was always a hit with the younger ones. There were many squeals of excitement when kids could see their pictures on the screen of my camera. These are the days when I love what I do, and it puts everything in perspective. When you yourself become a kid, you get better grounded. You stop taking yourself and everything else so seriously. Open your eyes, slow down, smile, have some fun and go for walk. It's amazing what you can find when you just walk.

Vehicle traffic in Dhaka is a real problem and that is an understatement. To give you an example, I once took a local bus from Saderghat to Banani, which is about 12 km.

Now in any western city, covering that kind of distance should only take maybe 30 to 45 minutes, even on a bad day. Now imagine it taking 2½ to 3 hours, and that's any day in Dhaka. It gets even worse during Ramadan, when it took more like 90 minutes to go 3 km. Why didn't I just walk, you ask; and after those episodes, that's what I did. All this is maybe not so surprising, though, when you realize Dhaka has 15 million people inhabiting an area about half the size of Calgary, Alberta, which numbers just over one million.

One thing I did notice in Dhaka was the contrast between the wealthy and the less fortunate, especially in the financial district, called Gulshan 1 and 2. I lived about a kilometre from this area and walked through the main intersections daily. And every day, I would notice the same groups of people approaching vehicles that were stopped at the traffic lights. These individuals would be trying to sell everything from balloons to stickers to maps and even using their own children and elderly, hoping to play the sympathy card. You would also see people with severe deformities and mental disabilities begging at the side of the road. Some are on their own, some are homeless, and surprisingly some even go to school. I was curious and decided to find out more about these people. That's when I met 11-year-old Rubina, who attends school during the day but comes to Gulshan 2 to beg for money from 4–10 p.m. almost every day. When I asked why, she told me, "Dad has no work and mum is gone. I need to take care of dad, he is sick."

I heard many similar stories from people who beg in Gulshan. I met Irene, for example, a mother of three children whose husband works as a rickshaw driver. She had been recently arrested because the police started cracking down on people begging in Gulshan 1 and 2. Irene told me she would be staying home until the police situation calmed down.

I made my way down to Sadarghat, the ferry slip in Dhaka, where you can get an overnight boat that is just a steel hull with 30 to 50 cabins depending on which vessel you catch. The ferry sails at 8 p.m. and arrives at about 5 the next morning. I was heading to a town called Barisal, and the overnight river trip was actually quite enjoyable. Given the heat, the fan in my little five-by-ten-foot cabin did its job and I was able to get five hours sleep. Once I arrived in Barisal, I checked into a cheap hotel for a whopping 300 taka (about C$4.25) a night, which included my own bathroom, single bed, little couch, a fan and a window to let in the morning light. Not exactly the Ritz, but who said photography was glamorous?

I managed to catch up on some sleep and then headed out for the day to photograph locals working the docks where all the cargo boats come in. Photographing in rural Bangladesh can be a challenge, as I quickly found out. Tourism is non-existent and the only foreigners Bengalis see are usually in the big cities like Dhaka or Chittagong working for NGOs and aid organizations. So when you are spotted in small villages and towns, people flock to you. Within minutes you'll have attracted a crowd that can range from 10 to 100 people. When you're trying to get candid images, you need to be on your toes to capture those moments. You are forced to constantly move around, even coming back to some subjects three or four times, trying to escape your retinue. After my day in Barisal I went back to my hotel, dropped off my gear, got some street food, had the best $1 haircut of my life and came back to relax with *Long Walk to Freedom: The Autobiography of Nelson Mandela*.

The next morning, I was up at six, grabbed my gear, paid my hotel bill and took a rickshaw to the docks to catch the seven o'clock boat for the two-hour ride to Bhola Island. The trip was a beautiful little cruise past riverside villages where locals were fishing, washing their cattle and going about their daily life in rural Bangladesh. Arriving on Bhola Island, I took an hour's bus ride to a town called Daulatkhan, where a very nice local by the name of Sonjoy offered to help in my search for the local fishing communities I was after. Sonjoy made a few calls, got me set up in a so-called guest house where I would be staying, and immediately took me to the local fishing authorities to discuss my plans. Needless to say the meeting went well and I was given permission to spend as many days with the fishermen as I liked. When I expressed my intention to stay aboard a fishing boat overnight, though, there was a slight concern due to the number of piracy incidents on the Meghna River recently.

Some fishermen had even been murdered for their catches and boats. Apparently, incidents had been occurring three or four times a month. The authorities said it would disgrace them if I were in any sort of danger and they did not want to take that chance. I respected their decision, but I was still a little upset I couldn't spend a few nights under the stars on the Meghna.

Over the next four days I had the opportunity to spend a day with captain Babu and his crew, visited numerous villages along the banks of the Meghna and went swimming in swamps. I had offers to join the local officers club (I don't know why, exactly, as I am not officer/corporate material). I was invited to meet the chairman of the district and spent 10 days with his family at their home. During that time, I got to experience a 35 mm 1970s Bengali action film in a makeshift theatre which itself looked like an abandoned building in a horror movie.

Over the final couple of weeks I went back to Bhola Island to spend more time with the fishermen and residents of the district. I only came back to Dhaka after my first visit because an opportunity arose for me to get access to the shipbreaking yards of Chittagong, though that later fell through due to the negative press the place had been getting all over the world.

My second trip to Bhola actually started out on a bizarre note. I left on the Friday so I would miss the weekend rush. (Since Bangladesh is 90 per cent Muslim, weekends are Friday and Saturday, so everyone travels on Thursday and returns to work on Sunday.) I hopped into a CNG, which is a motorized tricycle fuelled with compressed natural gas, with a metal frame and canvas covered compartment for the passenger behind the driver. We agreed on a price before I stepped into this rickety-looking machine, but halfway to Sadarghat to catch the overnight ferry my driver tells me he needs to get gas and that I have to pay for it on top of the fare we had

already agreed on. Laughing in his face I say no. He persists and I persist more. The arguing begins in earnest. So I unlatch the door of the CNG and get out, laughing out loud to let him know I'm not a fool and that I will simply go find a new ride without paying for this one. I'd barely walked 100 metres when my incensed CNG driver hauls up beside me and bounds furiously out of his vehicle. I notice now his hands have become fists, his teeth are clenched and he is puffed up like a cobra ready to strike. A little taken back, I immediately make myself look bigger, which is pretty easy for a tallish North American among smallish South Asians, and bear down on him, calling his bluff. I stop four inches from his face and point to my face, daring him to take the first swing. He immediately backs off, and as I turn around I notice we have already attracted an audience. Suddenly a Bengali kid no more than 18 years old asks me in very good English, "Is there a problem?" I tell him the situation and he responds by telling me that my driver wants me to pay for his gas as well as the fare, something I already knew. After about 20 minutes the CNG driver, the young English-speaking Bengali, a group of random men and myself are all still arguing loudly. Momentarily their focus is off me and I notice another CNG driver trying to get my attention from the side of the road, motioning for me to get into his vehicle. I casually approach him without the quarrelling group even noticing. We agree on a price and off we go before the group even notices I'm gone. When we arrive in Sadarghat, I pay the driver, buy my ticket for the overnight launch and set sail at 7:30 p.m. What an evening's entertainment.

I am awakened at 4 a.m. and told we have reached Barisal and I must immediately get off the ferry, as they still have three more hours of river to cover to reach the town where the remaining passengers are going. Stumbling across the deck and onto the gangway exhausted, I walk into Barisal to the same small hotel I had stayed at on my first visit. I crash

on their lobby couch, as I had to be awake in barely two hours to catch another ferry to Bhola Island. At six o'clock I actually manage to wake up and am graciously informed by the hotel owner that he won't be charging me for using his couch. I gratefully thank him and walk back to the docks to catch the first ferry of the morning. Seven o'clock comes around and we're off to Bhola. Still exhausted from the previous night's lack of sleep I immediately pass out and the two-hour ride becomes a blur. Around 9:30 I am awakened by a Bengali man poking me, as everyone has already started disembarking. Still half asleep, I trudge off the boat and board a local bus that will take me to Bhola station, where I will transfer to another bus that will take me again to Daulatkhan. Two hours later I arrive and I get the exact room I stayed in on my first visit.

By now it's about 11:30 and I slowly start to unpack. I had the mobile numbers of some of the fishing officials I'd met on my first visit, so I decide to call a few of them. After a few short conversations and not even an hour later there is a knock at the door and it's Ratan, the chairman of the district of Bhola. We have a few laughs and he immediately invites me to stay at his home, only a few kilometres east of Daulatkhan. I tell him I'd already planned to stay where I am for the first night but I will accept his invitation and see him the very next day. I spent the rest of the day reading, walking around town and visiting a few of the tea stalls I knew from my first visit, laughing and enjoying the locals' company and having large groups of Bengalis follow me around while being asked fifty times in two minutes what country I am from.

At around 9 p.m. and completely exhausted from the trip to Daulatkhan, I decide it's time to finally get a good night's sleep. I put my headphones in my ears and listen to *The Debaters* on CBC web radio for an hour until I slowly drift off to sleep. At around 11 I wake up suddenly to weird scratching noises. I barely notice some moving object in the dark but it looks about the size of my forearm. I turn on my headlamp and three inches from my face, with only a mosquito net separating the two of us, is a rat. I honestly thought I was still dreaming. In an instant the rat jumps away and hides somewhere under the bed. I quickly place my pillow at the other end of the bed and realize that this is not going to be a quiet night. So I pick up my book and start to read. Suddenly again there are noises and I see this rodent starting to climb the side of the bed. It scurries across the headboard and jumps onto the windowsill and out the window. I'm on the second floor of this building and there is nothing but a five-metre drop beyond the window shutters. Thirty minutes later the little beast jumps back in the window and scurries back under the bed. By now I'm actually kind of curious as to what this thing is doing. This same routine goes on for another hour and I still can't sleep. So after the third time the rat heads outside to god only knows where, I quickly close the shutters and immediately praise my quick thinking, out loud of course, that I have outsmarted a rat. Twenty minutes later I hear chewing noises on the shutters from the outside. Now I could just put my music back on to ignore the stupid thing but with 15 hours a day without power for the next 12 days, I can't be wasting all my iPod battery life on my first night because of a stupid rat. I punched the shutter with my fist cursing out loud. Finally there is silence.

The next morning I wake up to knocking at the door. Still extremely tired after a very restless night even after the rat incident was over, I open the door to one of Ratan's friends saying it's time to go. Still trying to wake up, I gather my things and head out. I pay for the room, jump on a rickshaw with this man named Jamal and proceed to Ratan's home three kilometres outside Daulatkhan. On arrival, I am greeted by Ratan, his family and his daughter's family and we all have breakfast together. After breakfast Ratan shows me to my room, which is more or less the same as the previous place I stayed at in Daulatkhan, and I start to unpack and get settled in for the next seven days.

During my 12 days in rural southern Bangladesh I photographed fishing villages, met village elders, politicians and NGO leaders and had some amazing encounters with Bengali people. I would be lying if I said it went smoothly and that everything was happy go lucky good times. But as the culture, mentalities and customs are completely different from what I am used to in the western world, this will give you an idea of daily life in rural Bangladesh. I would have random people just barge into my room and stare at me for no reason, taking photos with their phones, touching my equipment and not leaving when asked. It would bother me when people would question my character and intentions because of my religious beliefs or education background. The most frustrating thing was being severely taken advantage of when it came to the price of anything I tried to purchase, to the point where it was insulting. The attitude essentially was "you're white, so you're rich." I know people stare because they are curious. I know it's hard to convince people that it's okay not to believe in a religion and that a university degree is not what makes a person who they are. And yes, they see an opportunity to make some extra cash. But hey, it's a poor country, and if some foreigner can put more food on the table, then I guess I would probably do the same if I were in their situation. But at the end of the day the constant struggle wears you out mentally and it becomes a real challenge trying to convince yourself of this every time it happens, and it happens at least a dozen times a day.

It's funny, though, how an unpleasant experience can turn into good one. On one particular occasion, the son of the maid, a 9-year-old boy that helps his mother cook, clean and run errands for Ratan, was sitting on my bed staring at me – surprise, surprise. My wallet was next to him and I was directly across from him reading my book. As I looked up his hands were on my wallet trying to pry it open ever so slowly. Our eyes met and he quickly pulled his hands away. I immediately stood up and the kid went running out the door before I could open my mouth. I went to Ratan and told him what had happened, as my patience was already thin enough after all these random strangers visiting my room an hour before. The little boy got a small spanking from both his mother and Ratan. After a few hours I managed to cool down, and over the seven days the little boy, Siraj, and I went from being arch-enemies to playing hide and seek, scaring each other at every possible opportunity at night and building homemade helicopters with batteries, a mini-rotor, a pen, a paper clip and a couple of wires. I couldn't help but like this kid, as I used to do the same mischievous things when I was his age, so I bought him a lunghi (a sarong for men), which he was super-stoked about and wore the final day I was on the island.

On another day, Ratan organized a boat trip out to an island called Char Hazipur, where the residents were facing a few major problems. Ratan and I, along with a group of other Bengali men, boarded a wooden vessel and headed out to the island. The boat ride alone took about an hour where we travelled about 15 km to get to our final destination. When we arrived at Char Hazipur, I was completely shocked at what I saw. The people on this particular char in the middle of the Meghna River were living in some of the worst conditions I had ever seen. Their low-lying island homes had no protection from the storm surges that hit this region of south Bangladesh every year. Residents were literally living among their livestock, sleeping and living in animal waste. Their water source was severely polluted and they were drinking raw river water. On top of all this, half their cattle had died due to unexplained causes. The elderly villagers said that within a week after the vet had delivered vaccines for their cattle, the animals started rapidly dying off. After witnessing all this I don't think I have ever contemplated my own, relatively privileged situation in life more than I did after that day. I don't mean to preach, but this is why I always encourage people to travel in order to experience what others' lives are like and really think about your own. Be thankful you can afford a car and live in a comfortable country where you have a paved road to drive on and a job to travel to and from at your own convenience.

After Bhola Island I decided to travel to Kuakata, as everyone had good things to say about this little beach town. Needing a little R 'n' R, I decided it would be a great opportunity to also photograph some Bangladesh beach life.

After three days in Kuakata, I decided it was time to head back to Dhaka, as I would be starting a little part-time job teaching hip hop at an international school for kids aged 7–17. I was to take a night bus, leaving at 5 p.m. and arriving in Dhaka at 5 or 6 the next morning.

I made the bus in plenty of time, but just as we were ready to pull out, the motor refused to start. After 20 minutes a tractor pulls up and starts to push us from behind in hopes of roll-starting the bus, since it has a standard transmission. Finally, after several pushes, the motor kicks over and we're off. The first two hours of the ride was spent jouncing over a maze of potholes on a road covered with two feet of mud. We were barely making 50 km/h. After the bumpy bit we finally hit some decent pavement/compressed dirt where the bus picked up speed and we started to leave some distance behind us.

In Bangladesh there are many rivers and not very many bridges, so in order to cross the water you need ferries. The trip back to Dhaka included five ferry rides, one of which included a four-hour delay before we could even board. The final crossing, though, was the worst. The tugboat that was moving the ferry barge on its port side suddenly gave way. Everything happened so fast and all I could see were cables flying past the bus like whips and this sense of drifting as the tug pulled away from the barge. The barge, carrying six full-size buses, suddenly started to go out of control towards the aft section and the entire vessel started to list dramatically to starboard, causing the buses to almost lean against one another like dominoes. I nearly shit my pants and was ready to jump ship. Amid the chaos on the ferry, our bus driver managed to cause two accidents, two fistfights and two flat tires and do the most erratic driving I have ever experienced on any bus in any country. Not to mention the transmission, which literally fell out from under the bus on the last 20 km back to Dhaka. When that happened, I just walked away calmly, too tired to get upset, and flagged another bus. By this time it had taken 20 hours to cover 350 kilometres. Naturally, there was no air conditioning or even fans on the bus, amid 35° temperatures, so I got no sleep whatsoever. Once I arrived in Dhaka, all I wanted was a nice coffee from my favourite shop. Not surprisingly, however, and now that I was going into my twenty-fourth hour awake ... the place was closed. The one thing I craved after such an ordeal I could not even have! It was time to admit defeat, as I was mentally and physically exhausted. The moment I got home to my apartment I had a cold bucket shower, put on clean clothes and went to bed chuckling to myself, knowing this was one experience I would never forget and always cherish.

Travelling does that to us, or rather, for us. It pushes us, makes us uncomfortable. It humbles the stubbornest of individuals. It forces us to adapt, to conquer goals both big and small. Why do we do it? The only way to answer that is to go and get yourself lost.

OFF THE BEATEN PATH

Tips to take you out of your comfort zone and make travel that much more exciting and genuine

I must confess that before I left on this adventure, I purchased a guidebook for each of the countries I would be visiting. Once I arrived in Nepal, though, I realized this was just a waste of money. Guidebooks are great if all you want to do is sightsee, visit the temples and not think, while allowing a book to tell you where to eat and sleep and how to say "hello" and "thank you" in a foreign language. But if you're looking for a bit of grittiness and a real challenge when travelling abroad, please control your urge to buy a guidebook. You will thank yourself after the trip is done, when you're on the plane ride home.

Here's a quick list compiled from my own personal experience of travelling in both developed and undeveloped countries.

· **Research** whatever aspect of your destinations you are interested in (food, history, geography, culture etc.). Obviously, Google and your local library are good places to start. It may also be useful to contact people from community organizations that might give you an insider's perspective, such as ethnic or immigrant associations or aid agencies, for example.

· *Be genuine about your intentions:* If you're going to Thailand to solicit women or men or children, I hope you end up in a Thai prison. Treat others and the environments you visit as if they were your own family and home.

· *Volunteer* for local organizations in your destination countries. This is by far the best way to contribute. It also is a great opportunity to meet locals and other international volunteers, and you never know what other opportunities and adventures this will lead to.

· *Languages:* Learn basic greetings and phrases in the languages of the places you will be visiting. Knowing even a few words in the local dialect can go a long way to at least start communication.

- *Always smile*, especially when you greet someone.
- *Maps:* Whether before you leave or after you arrive, obtain an up-to-date, detailed map of the places you want to visit. (Again, Google is a great place to start.)
- *Accommodation:* Staying in backpacker/tourist places is perfectly fine, but if you don't like noise, ask a local where they would recommend you stay. You never know, they might even invite you to stay with their family.
- *Avoid the beaten track:* Try travelling in the opposite direction from where most people go, which is on organized tours and popular trails. Some of my favourite places, where I would end up staying for weeks, I discovered by just getting on a bus, then a boat, then another bus, and staying on it, sometimes for days, until the end of the line!
- *Music:* Make sure you have lots of music, as this can save your sanity when on long bus rides, walks or even the sleepless nights where all you hear is honking and stray dogs barking. Also try and find local music that fits your taste.
- *Use common sense:* You know the saying "common sense is not all that common"? Try walking with confidence, and always look like you know where you are going. Even if you get lost it's not hard to hail a taxi and ask for directions. Trust your gut *always*, as this can be the start of some amazing experiences and save you heaps of trouble and a possible wrong encounter.
- *Transit:* Use public transit or rent a bike. Some of my favourite travel experiences came from just hopping on a bike, as it is a great way to see a city or town close-up and at a very leisurely pace.
- *Food:* Eat the local cuisine and *always* try the street food. I always see guidebooks advising travellers to stay away from street food, but I believe the best food is on the street. Just eat at stalls frequented by locals and eat when the locals eat. Use your common sense and bon appétit!
- *Be open-minded:* Try new things, get out of your comfort zone and push yourself to do things you wouldn't normally do.

NEPAL
PORTRAITS & ENCOUNTERS

THIS MAN WAS PART OF A CREW OF FOUR DIGGING A WELL BY HAND AT SURKHET.
WATER SHORTAGES ARE COMMON IN NEPAL'S DRY SEASON, AND THE ORGANIZATION
I WAS VOLUNTEERING FOR (BLINKNOW.ORG) DECIDED TO PITCH IN TO HELP.

A YOUNG BOY SUDDENLY FORGETS WHY HE WAS CRYING
AS HE SPOTS ME TAKING HIS PHOTOGRAPH.

THIS YOUNG GIRL BY THE NAME OF BUSHANTI ALLOWED ME TO TAKE HER PORTRAIT IN FRONT OF HER HOME IN SIMIKOT IN THE FAR NORTHWEST NEPAL REGION OF HUMLA.

THE VIEW FROM THE FRONT DOOR OF MY TENT IN THE SMALL VILLAGE OF BURGAUN. THIS PLACE IS 10 DAYS WALK FROM THE CLOSEST ROAD OR YOU CAN CATCH A FLIGHT TO SIMIKOT AND HIKE 4–5 HOURS. THE VILLAGE CALLED THEHE IS CENTRE FRAME FAR IN THE DISTANCE.

THE PARENTS OF THESE CHILDREN ALLOWED ME TO CAMP ON
THE ROOF OF THEIR HOME IN BURGAUN. YOU CAN SEE ONE OF
THE CHILDREN BLOWING THROUGH A PIECE OF BAMBOO TO GET
THE FIRE GOING SO THEY CAN BOIL WATER AND COOK FOOD.

HERE'S THE WHOLE FAMILY.

A ELDERLY WOMAN PEERS OUT HER WINDOW IN KATHMANDU.

TWO NEPALI BOYS POSE FOR A PORTRAIT ON TOP OF MOUNDS OF GARBAGE WHICH
THEY PLAN TO SIFT THROUGH TO RECYCLE AND SELL WHAT THEY CAN.

A NEPALI MOTHER, CHILD AND GRANDMOTHER ALLOW ME TO PHOTOGRAPH
THEM ALONG THE BANKS OF THE BAGMATI RIVER IN KATHMANDU, NEPAL.

A GROUP OF NEPALI MEN POSE FOR A PHOTOGRAPH FIRST THING IN THE MORNING.

A YOUNG GIRL QUIETLY WAKES BEHIND THE MOSQUITO NETTING THAT
PROTECTS HER FAMILY OF SIX IN THEIR SMALL HOME IN KATHMANDU.

A FAMILY QUIETLY WAKES UP AND ALLOWS ME TO
PHOTOGRAPH THEM IN THEIR HOME IN KATHMANDU.

A YOUNG BOY TAKES OVER AT HIS FAMILY'S VEGETABLE STAND IN
THE LOCAL MARKET WHILE HIS MOTHER CATCHES SOME SLEEP.

A NEPALI MOTHER HELPING HER DAUGHTER DO HER HOMEWORK
BEFORE SHE LEAVES FOR SCHOOL THAT MORNING.

AN ELDERLY WOMAN BEGS FOR MONEY IN
THE SMALL TOWN OF BHAKTAPUR, NEPAL.

A YOUNG BOY AND HIS FATHER RUNNING THEIR
VEGETABLE STAND IN A KATHMANDU MARKET.

A YOUNG BOY ALLOWS ME TO TAKE HIS PORTRAIT IN
ONE OF THE MANY LARGE MARKETS IN KATHMANDU.

THIS ELDERLY WOMAN IN
BHAKTAPUR AGREED TO SIT FOR
HER PORTRAIT. WHEN I SHOWED
HER THE PHOTOGRAPH, SHE MADE
A FACE AS IF TO SAY IT WAS NOT
UP TO HER EXPECTATIONS. WE
BOTH HAD A GOOD LAUGH.

A NEPALI METALWORKER
POSES FOR A PORTRAIT...

...AND HAS SOME FUN WITH THE IDEA.

A NEPALI WORKER BRUSHING HIS TEETH BEFORE STARTING HIS DAY
MAKING METAL BOWLS THAT WILL BE SOLD IN THE LOCAL MARKETS.

A GROUP PICTURE WITH SOME OF THE METALWORKERS I HAD THE
PRIVILEGE OF PHOTOGRAPHING. EACH ONE OF THEM RECEIVED
THEIR OWN PORTRAIT PLUS IMAGES OF THEM WORKING.

AN ELDERLY NEPALI FARMER CHECKS HIS CROPS
NEAR A VILLAGE OUTSIDE KATHMANDU.

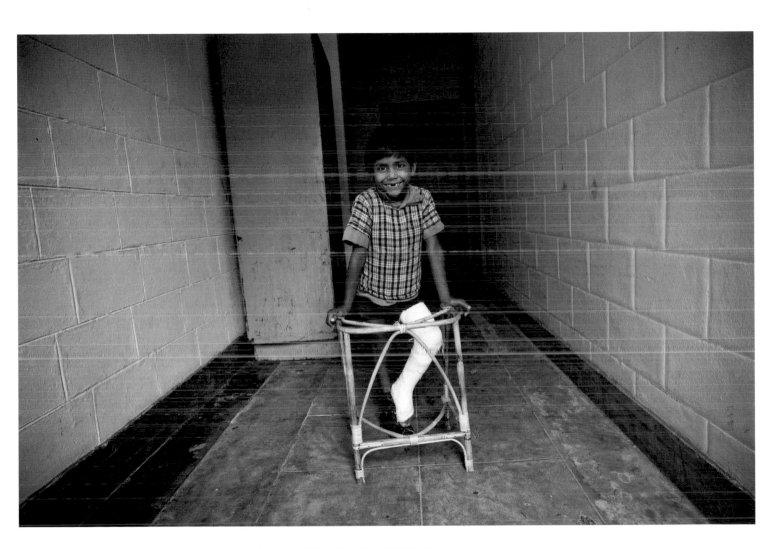

A YOUNG BOY POSES FOR HIS PHOTOGRAPH AT THE HOSPITAL AND
REHABILITATION CENTRE FOR CHILDREN WITH DISABILITIES.

BRICKYARDS

TWO NEPALI MEN BETWEEN THE
SMOKESTACKS OF THE KILN THAT
FIRES THE RAW CLAY IN THE
BRICKWORKS AT SURKHET, NEPAL.

A PORTRAIT OF SARSURSAH
MOHAMMED, WHO WORKS IN THE
BRICKYARDS AT SURKHET.

A YOUNG GIRL TOSSING FINISHED BRICKS OUT OF
THE KILN PIT. FROM HERE THE BRICKS WILL BE
TAKEN TO MARKET FOR USE IN CONSTRUCTION.

A YOUNG GIRL POSES FOR A PORTRAIT IN
THE BRICKYARDS AT SURKHET, NEPAL.

A YOUNG GIRL ASSEMBLES A STACK OF BRICKS TO LOAD
ON HER HEADSLING AND CARRY TO A WAITING TRUCK.

TEENAGE GIRLS HAULING CURED BRICKS OUT OF
THE KILN PIT AND CARRYING THEM TO A TRANSPORT
TRUCK. EACH BRICK WEIGHS ABOUT 2 KILOS.

HAULING A LOAD OF BRICKS WITH A HEADSLING.

A YOUNG GIRL CARRYING A LOAD
OF BRICKS TO A SEPARATE PILE
SOME 20 METRES AWAY.

A YOUNG GIRL'S HAND ADDING ONE MORE BRICK TO
THE 10 OR SO ALREADY STACKED ON HER HEAD.

A NEPALI MAN POSES FOR A PHOTO
AMONGST LARGE CHUNKS OF THE
COAL THAT FUELS THE BRICK KILN.

A GROUP OF MEN DOING THEIR DAILY CHORES WHERE THEY LIVE AND
WORK AMONGST THE BRICKYARDS NEAR BHAKTAPUR, NEPAL.

THIS PHOTOGRAPH SHOWS THE AMOUNT OF BRICKS ONE FACILITY CAN
PRODUCE. THE RECTANGULAR STRUCTURE ON TOP IS WHERE THE
WORKERS LIVE 8–9 MONTHS OF THE YEAR. THE REMAINING 3–4 MONTHS
IS THE RAINY SEASON, WHEN PRODUCTION STOPS COMPLETELY.

CAMERA-SHY ATOP THE IMMENSE INVENTORY
OF PRODUCT AT THE BRICKWORKS.

A YOUNG WOMAN SHOWS OFF HER BABY WHERE SHE LIVES
AND WORKS IN THE BRICKYARDS IN BHAKTAPUR.

THIS WOMAN WAS ONE OF THE FEW I ENCOUNTERED WHO
ACTUALLY APPROACHED ME AND ASKED TO HAVE HER PHOTO
TAKEN. I WAS HONOURED, GIVEN HER RADIANT SMILE.

A YOUNG BOY PLAYFULLY WALKS AMONGST THE
VAST STACKS OF PRODUCT WHILE HIS PARENT WORK
IN THE BRICKYARDS AT BHAKTAPUR, NEPAL.

LIVING QUARTERS AT THE BHAKTAPUR BRICKYARD.

A YOUNG GIRL TRYING TO KEEP WARM AS IT STARTS TO RAIN. SHE LIVES
WITH HER PARENTS AT THE BRICKWORKS IN BHAKTAPUR, NEPAL.

A NEPALI FATHER SHOWS OFF HIS TWIN BABIES.

A NEPALI MAN POSES FOR A PORTRAIT WHILE WORKING IN THE BRICKYARDS.

A LITTLE GIRL POSES FOR A PORTRAIT IN THE
BRICKYARDS WHERE SHE LIVES WITH HER FAMILY.

A LITTLE PIECE OF HEAVEN

AN ELDERLY MAN READING IN AFTERNOON LIGHT IN THE
PASHUPATINATH ASHRAM. HE GLANCED AT ME ONCE,
SMILED CONTENTLY AND WENT BACK TO HIS BOOK.

IN A DARK CORRIDOR OF THE ASHRAM, A MAN SITS PENSIVELY
IN MORNING LIGHT. I LIKE TO BELIEVE HE WAS JUST
ENJOYING THE PEACEFULNESS OF HIS OWN THOUGHTS.

THIS LADY ALWAYS HAD A SMILE ON HER FACE AND A CIGARETTE IN HER HAND. WHETHER I WAS HELPING WITH DAILY HOUSEKEEPING OR TAKING HER PHOTOGRAPH, SHE WAS AN ABSOLUTE DELIGHT AND MADE A JOYFUL IMPRESSION ON EVERYONE AT THE ASHRAM.

THIS MAN RARELY SAID ANYTHING,
SMOKED HIS CIGARETTES
CASUALLY AND ALWAYS WORE
HIS TOWERING TUQUE.

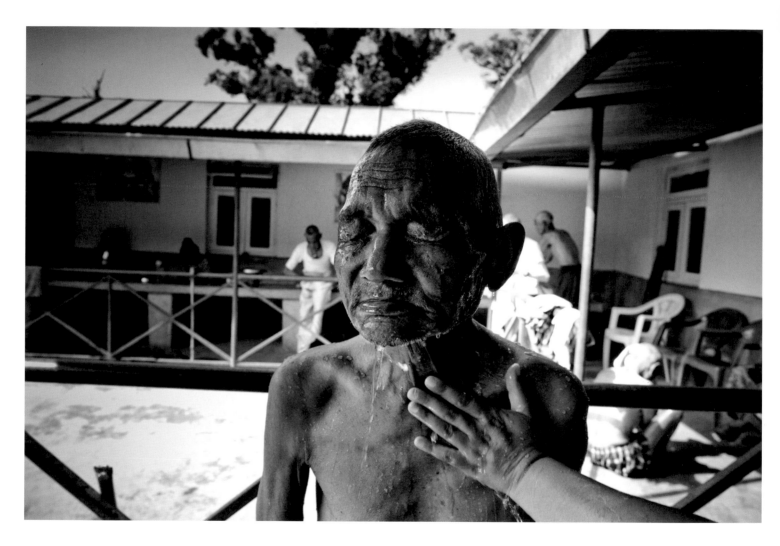

SOME ASHRAM RESIDENTS DETESTED BATH TIME. OTHERS WOULD
CRAVE THE EXPERIENCE OF BEING TOUCHED BY SOMEONE AND YOU
COULD SEE IN THEIR FACES HOW MUCH IT AFFECTED THEM.

A NEPALI VOLUNTEER WASHES ONE OF THE ELDERLY WOMEN.

AN ELDERLY WOMAN WAITS PATIENTLY
FOR VOLUNTEERS TO BATHE HER.

OCCASIONALLY THE GENERAL PUBLIC VISITS THE ASHRAM
TO HAND OUT FRUIT, JUICE BOXES AND SWEETS. RESIDENTS'
SPIRITS ARE LIFTED, ESPECIALLY IF IT'S BATH DAY AS WELL.

A GROUP OF WOMEN RESIDENTS ENJOY
THE SUN AFTER A MEAL OF DAL BHAT.

THIS ELDERLY MAN RECEIVES A LITTLE EXTRA
CARE DUE TO THE LOSS OF HIS LEFT LEG.

SOME ASHRAM RESIDENTS ARE ABLE TO
WASH THEMSELVES WITHOUT ASSISTANCE.

AN ELDERLY WOMAN TAKES AN AFTERNOON NAP AFTER
A BATH, LUNCH AND SOME TIME IN THE SUNSHINE.

WATCHING THE MEN BEING BATHED ONCE
A WEEK WAS QUITE THE EVENT.

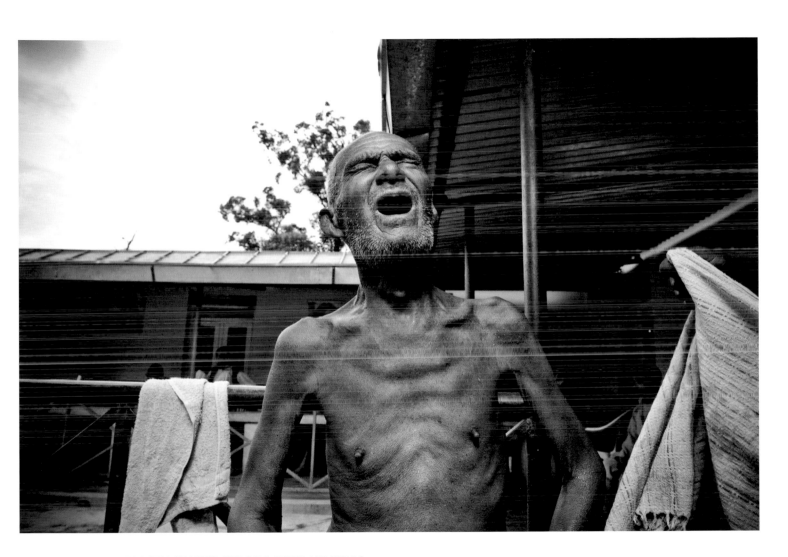

THIS FELLOW HATED THE COLD WATER AND WOULD
THROW TEMPER TANTRUMS LIKE A CHILD BEING
FORCED TO DO SOMETHING HE DID NOT WANT TO DO.

TWO RESIDENTS WAIT THEIR TURN TO BE BATHED BY VOLUNTEERS.

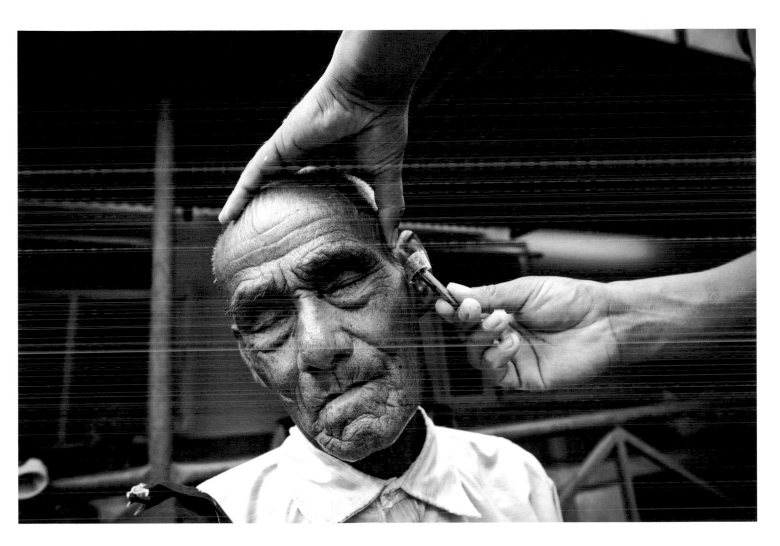

WHEN THE MEN'S WHISKERS START TO GET A LITTLE SHAGGY, LOCAL
VOLUNTEERS VISIT THE ASHRAM TO GIVE THEM A CLEAN SHAVE.

THIS ELDERLY WOMAN IS BLIND AND ALMOST DEAF. SHE
WAITS PATIENTLY TO BE BATHED BY LOCAL VOLUNTEERS.

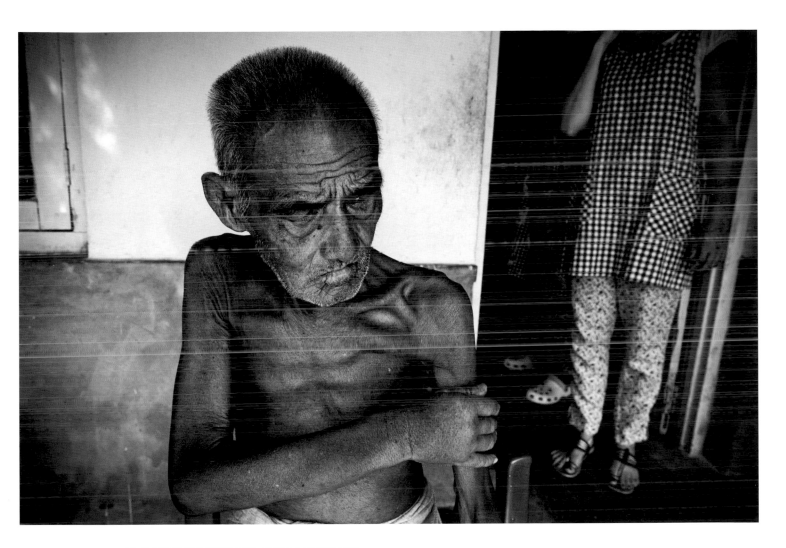

AN ELDERLY RESIDENT SITS QUIETLY IN THE SUN.

THIS MAN SEEMED TO ENJOY SITTING ON THE TABLE WHERE
MOST OF THE RESIDENTS DINE. HE WOULD JUST PERCH
THERE AND STARE SILENTLY LIKE A BIRD ON A WIRE.

PASHUPATINATH ASHRAM RESIDENTS SITTING
QUIETLY AFTER THEIR AFTERNOON MEAL.

AFTER I HAD SHOT A FEW FRAMES OF THIS FELLOW
AND SHOWED HIM HIS IMAGE ON THE CAMERA'S
SCREEN, HE NEARLY FELL TO THE FLOOR LAUGHING.

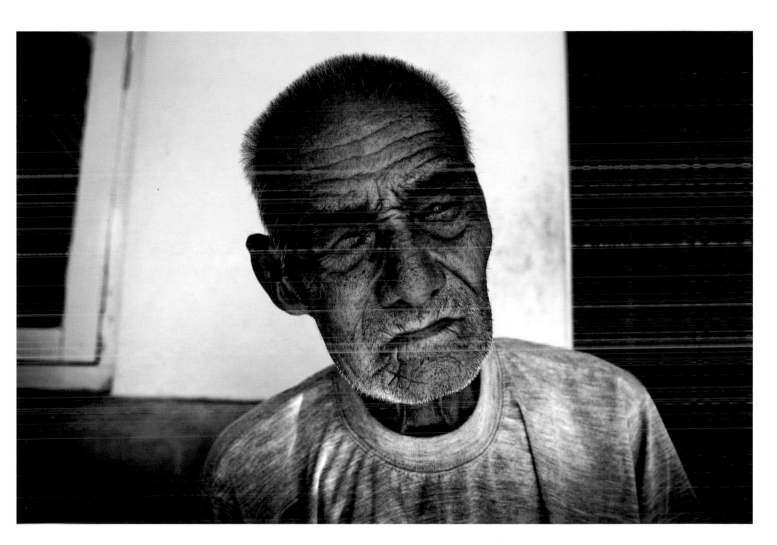

I COULDN'T HELP BUT MAKE A PORTRAIT
OF THIS MAN FOR THE DETAIL AND
CHARACTER IN HIS FACE.

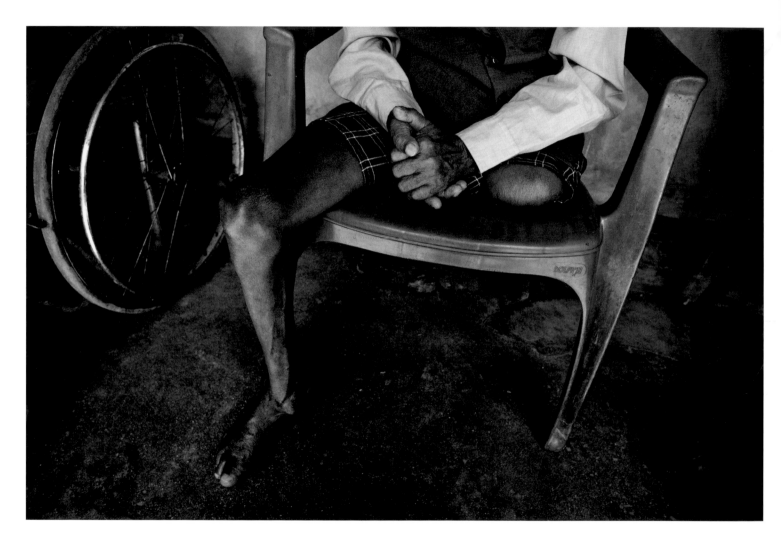

UNDER THE ASHRAM'S METAL AWNING, AN ELDERLY MAN
TAKES SHELTER FROM THE AFTERNOON HEAT.

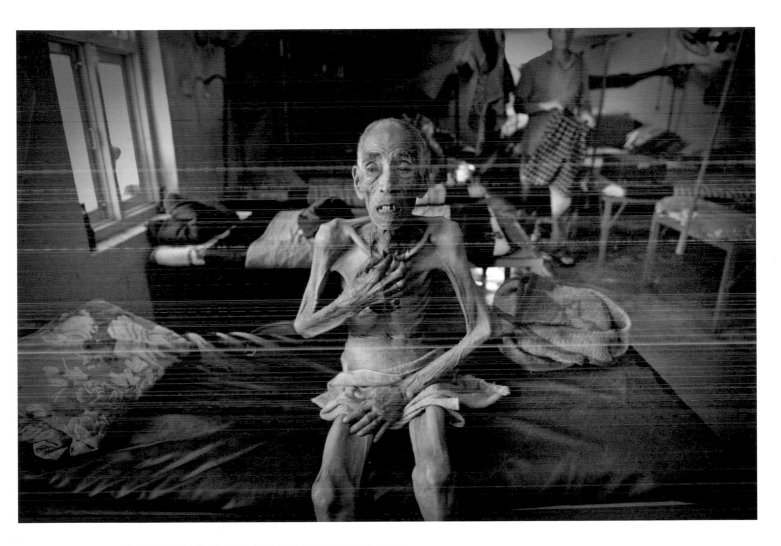

FROM WHAT I HEARD, THIS MAN WAS FOUND ON THE FRONT
STEPS THE NIGHT BEFORE I VISITED THE ASHRAM.

RICE, LENTILS AND OTHER VEGETABLES.

MOST ASHRAM RESIDENTS EAT WITH THEIR FINGERS AS
OTHER NEPALIS DO, BUT THIS MAN PREFERRED A SPOON.

ENJOYING AN AFTERNOON MEAL IN THE SHADE TO ESCAPE THE DRY-SEASON HEAT.

THIS WOMAN WAS BLIND AND SUBJECT TO UNCONTROLLABLE FITS OF SHOUTING AND FLAILING. AS I SAT WITH HER ONE DAY, SHE GRABBED MY HAND AND STARTED RUBBING MY ARM. INSTANTLY SHE CALMED, AS IF ALL SHE NEEDED WAS A LITTLE HUMAN CONTACT. WHEN I HAD TO GET BACK TO HELPING WITH ASHRAM CHORES, HER SPASMS RESUMED.

BANGLADESH
PORTRAITS & ENCOUNTERS

THIS YOUNG MAN SELLS FRUIT AT THE LARGE
PASSENGER FERRIES IN SADARGHAT, DHAKA.

WHAT IS NOW KNOWN AS "PHOTOBOMBING." THIS MAN DID NOT
KNOW THERE WAS SOMEONE BEHIND HIM AS I TOOK HIS PORTRAIT.

I STUMBLED ACROSS THIS GROUP OF KIDS GOING FOR A SWIM
DOWN BY THE DOCKS IN THE LITTLE TOWN OF BARISAL.

SOME OF THEM COULD FLY! OR SO IT MAY SEEM.

A MAN ON THE STREET IN BARISAL. HIS SKIN LOOKS ALMOST SCALY BECAUSE
OF ARSENIC POLLUTION IN GROUNDWATER. ALTHOUGH THERE HAS BEEN
MUCH IMPROVEMENT IN THIS THROUGHOUT RURAL BANGLADESH, MANY
ELDERLY PEOPLE WERE DANGEROUSLY EXPOSED TO THIS CONTAMINATION.

JUST ANOTHER FRIENDLY ENCOUNTER ON THE DOCKS IN BARISAL.
UNFORTUNATELY I DID NOT HAVE A TRANSLATOR WITH ME, SO I
COULDN'T ASK THIS FELLOW ABOUT THE SCARS ON HIS CHEST.

A SMALL BOY IN THE BEACH TOWN OF KUAKATA PULLS A
MAKESHIFT TOY BUILT FROM A PLASTIC BOTTLE, SOME WIRE
AND STRING, AND PIECES OF WOOD FOR WHEELS.

I STUMBLED UPON THESE TWO ONE EVENING AS THE FATHER WAS PREPARING TO GO FISHING. SOME KUAKATA FISHERMEN WILL STAY OUT ON THE WATER ALL NIGHT AND RETURN IN THE MORNING TO SELL THEIR CATCH WHEN THE MARKET OPENS. THEY DO THIS SIX NIGHTS A WEEK, SOMETIMES MAKING A SECOND TRIP IN THE AFTERNOON.

MY ENCOUNTER WITH A YOUNG CHILD AND HIS
MOTHER LATE ONE NIGHT IN GULSHAN 2, DHAKA.

I "SHOT FROM THE HIP" FOR THIS IMAGE, TRYING TO PHOTOGRAPH DISCREETLY
FOR ONCE. I CHOSE TO KEEP IT BECAUSE OF THE SUBJECT'S TENSION
THROUGH HIS BODY LANGUAGE AND HIS FOCUS AWAY FROM THE LENS.

A WONDERFUL AND PLAYFUL ENCOUNTER WITH A MOTHER
AND HER SON ON THE STREETS OF DHAKA IN GULSHAN 2.

THIS IMAGE IS ONE OF MY FAVOURITES BECAUSE
THE SLOGAN ON THE GIRL'S SHIRT SAYS SO MUCH.

A BOY LOOKS CURIOUSLY INTO THE CAMERA ON THE STREETS OF DHAKA.

THEN HE PLAYFULLY HIDES IN HIS MOTHER'S SARI.

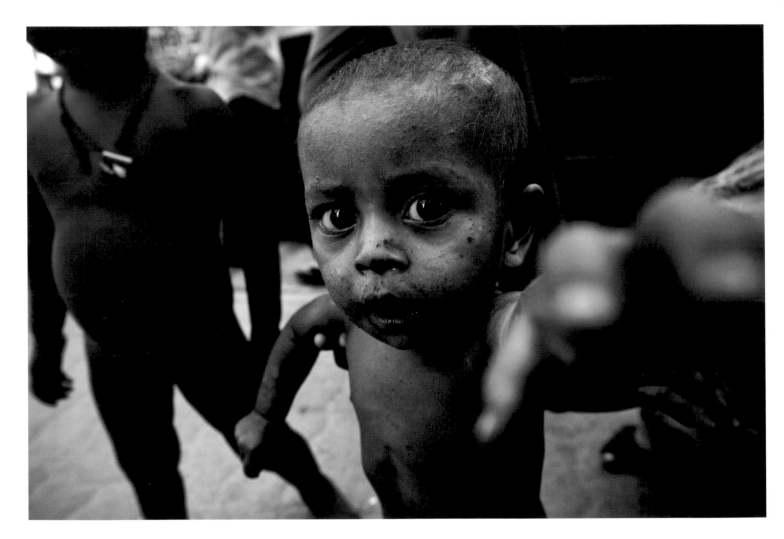

A YOUNG CHILD LETTING HIS CURIOSITY TAKE OVER. I DON'T
BLAME HIM. IF SOMEONE POINTED SOMETHING AT ME THAT
WAS SHINY AND WITHIN REACH, I'D GO FOR IT TOO.

ANOTHER CROSS-CULTURAL SHIRT.

A BOY CALMLY WALKING THE TRACKS IN HIS NEIGHBOURHOOD
AMONGST THE PASSING TRAINS IN DHAKA.

A GROUP OF BOYS PLAYING THE POPULAR BOARD
GAME CARROM RIGHT ON THE TRAIN TRACKS.

A YOUNG BOY POSES FOR A PORTRAIT WHERE HE LIVES,
ONLY A FEW FEET FROM THE TRAINS THAT PASS EVERY DAY.
I LATER LEARNED HE'D LOST HIS FOOT IN A BUS ACCIDENT.

THIS BENGALI LADY ALLOWED ME TO TAKE HER PORTRAIT IN
DHAKA. BEHIND HER IS THE SHOP WHERE SHE MAKES SPARKLERS,
A TYPE OF DECORATIVE CANDLES USED ON BIRTHDAY CAKES.

THIS YOUNG GIRL AND ELDERLY WOMAN WERE VERY CURIOUS ABOUT MY GEAR AS I WAS WALKING THE RAIL LINES IN DHAKA. WHEN I SHOWED THEM THEIR PICTURE ON THE CAMERA SCREEN, THE LADY IMMEDIATELY WANTED ME TO TAKE ANOTHER WITH JUST HERSELF.

SO HERE SHE IS.

A YOUNG BOY WALKS BETWEEN CARS STOPPED AT A RED LIGHT
IN DHAKA'S GULSHAN 2 DISTRICT. HE KNOCKS ON DRIVERS'
WINDOWS IN HOPES OF GETTING FOOD OR MONEY.

I MET RUBINA IN GULSHAN 2, WHERE SHE SPENDS HER DAYS IN SCHOOL AND
IN THE EVENINGS ASKS FOR MONEY FROM PASSING CARS AND PEDESTRIANS.
IT TURNS OUT HER FATHER IS ILL AND SHE USES THE MONEY TO SUPPORT HIM.

HITCHING A RIDE ATOP A DHAKA TRAIN. THE BOY IN THE PHOTOGRAPH
IS 11 YEARS OLD AND DOES THIS EVERY DAY TO AND FROM WORK.

PEOPLE RIDE ON TOP OF THE TRAINS BECAUSE THEY CAN'T AFFORD THE
FARE, WHICH AMOUNTS TO ABOUT 50¢ TO 75¢ CANADIAN. THIS WAS A GREAT
EXPERIENCE, BUT I WOULD SUGGEST YOU EXERCISE EXTREME CAUTION.

A GROUP OF WORKERS FIXING THE HULLS OF
MID-SIZE BARGES IN DHAKA'S OLD QUARTER.

A LONE WORKER STANDING ON TOP OF
A BARGE IN DHAKA'S OLD QUARTER.

TAKING A WALK ALONG DHAKA'S TRAIN LINES
AND PHOTOGRAPHING PEOPLE I MEET.

THIS FATHER AND SON ALLOWED ME TO TAKE THEIR PICTURE
IN FRONT OF THEIR HOME ALONG THE RAILWAY.

A BOY AND HIS PALS, CURIOUS AS EVER.

TWO YOUNG BOYS POSE FOR A PHOTOGRAPH ALONG
THE DHAKA TRAIN LINE WHERE THEY LIVE.

ALWAYS A JOYFUL ENCOUNTER WHILE
GOING FOR A WALK IN DHAKA.

AN ELDERLY MAN WASHES HIMSELF IN THE BURIGANGA
RIVER, WHERE HE WORKS AMONGST THE BARGES.

I SPOTTED THIS BOY PLAYING IN THE SHIPYARD IN DHAKA'S
OLD QUARTER, LEAPING FROM TRACK TO TRACK WHERE
HUGE BARGES ARE LAUNCHED INTO THE BURIGANGA RIVER.

A WORKER ENJOYS A CIGARETTE AFTER A LONG SHIFT ON
THE BARGES. ON THIS PARTICULAR DAY THE TEMPERATURE
IN DHAKA REACHED A RECORD HIGH 42°C (108°F).

A BROTHER AND SISTER POSE FOR A PORTRAIT AT 2:30 A.M. IN DHAKA. THE GIRL ACTUALLY
STOPPED A GROUP OF MEN FROM TRYING TO STEAL MY GEAR AFTER OVERHEARING
THEM TALKING ABOUT IT. SHE MOTIONED TO ME, POINTING TO MY CAMERA THEN
TO THE MEN, WITH MULTIPLE CURSES IN BENGALI AND BROKEN ENGLISH.

A YOUNG BOY SITS ON HIS SISTER'S LAP IN THE BIHARI REFUGEE CAMP IN DHAKA.

A MOTHER PLAYFULLY HIDES HER FACE AS HER DAUGHTER VERY
CASUALLY POSES FOR A PORTRAIT IN THE BIHARI REFUGEE CAMP.

SISTERS ENJOYING HAVING THEIR PHOTOGRAPH
TAKEN IN THE REFUGEE CAMP.

THIS BOY TOOK TO ME THE MOMENT I SET FOOT IN THE BIHARI REFUGEE CAMP. HE SPOKE NO ENGLISH BUT INSISTED ON BEING MY VERY OWN PERSONAL TOUR GUIDE THROUGH THE CAMP. WHEN I FINALLY SAT DOWN FOR SOME CHAI, I NOTICED HIS SHIRT AND COULD NOT HELP BUT PHOTOGRAPH THIS JOYFUL LITTLE BOY AND THE IRREPRESSIBLE MESSAGE ON HIS SHIRT.

JUST HANGING OUT WITH THE LOCAL BOYS IN
THE BIHARI REFUGEE CAMP IN DHAKA.

A MAN ALLOWING ME TO TAKE HIS PORTRAIT
IN THE PABNA MENTAL INSTITUTION.

A MAN IS HELD IN CHAINS AS HIS AUNT AND MOTHER
WAIT FOR HIM TO BE ASSESSED AT PABNA'S MENTAL
INSTITUTION. THIS WAS HIS THIRD VISIT TO THE HOSPITAL.

A BENGALI MAN WORKING IN A BRICKYARD
JUST OUTSIDE PABNA, BANGLADESH.

A BENGALI MAN POSES FOR A PORTRAIT
IN THE PABNA BRICKYARDS.

A YOUNG GIRL ASLEEP ON THE STREET IN DHAKA.

JUST OUTSIDE DHAKA ABOUT 200 RESIDENTS HAVE CREATED RESERVOIRS TO FARM FISH IN THE WET SEASON AND CROPS IN THE DRY SEASON WHEN THE WATER RECEDES. EACH PERSON OWNS SHARES DEPENDING ON THEIR INITIAL INVESTMENT, AND PROFITS FROM THE SALES OF EACH CROP PRODUCED.

163

BHOLA ISLAND

A GROUP OF BENGALIS POSE FOR A PHOTO JUST
OUTSIDE OF DAULATKHAN, ON THE MEGHNA
RIVER IN SOUTHERN BANGLADESH.

SILHOUETTE OF A YOUNG FISHERMAN ALONG THE MEGHNA.

A FISHERMAN GLADLY STOPS WORKING FOR A MOMENT TO HAVE HIS
PORTRAIT TAKEN ALONG THE BANKS OF THE MEGHNA RIVER.

A FISHERMAN'S NET AND HANDS.

ON MY ARRIVAL IN DAULATKHAN I WAS GREETED BY THREE PEOPLE.
WITHIN THIRTY MINUTES I HAD ATTRACTED QUITE A CROWD.

A LOCAL FISHERMAN
POSES FOR A PORTRAIT.

A YOUNG BOY WHO WORKS FULL
TIME ABOARD A FISHING VESSEL
POSES FOR A PORTRAIT.

I WAS ALLOWED TO SPEND THE DAY WITH A FISHING
CREW ON THE MEGHNA RIVER. THE HAND ON
THE TILLER IS THAT OF CAPTAIN BABU.

CAPTAIN BABU'S FISHING CREW.

ONE OF THE CREW QUIETLY LISTENS TO THE RADIO
AS WE WAIT FOR THE NETS TO FILL WITH FISH.

A PORTRAIT OF A
BENGALI FISHERMAN.

THIS YOUNG BOY WORKS ON THE FISHING BOAT
FULL TIME, LEARNING THE TRADE, MENDING NETS
AND HELPING TO GET THE CATCH TO MARKET.

HAULING IN THE FIRST CATCH OF THE DAY.

THIS YOUNG BOY PLAYFULLY
HANGS OFF THE BOW AS THE
BOAT HEADS IN TO DROP OFF
THE CATCH AT THE DOCKS.

A WORKER TAKES A SILENT BREAK IN THE HOLD OF A BOAT HE IS HELPING TO
BUILD WITH THE FISHING COMMUNITY JUST OUTSIDE OF DAULATKHAN. ONCE
THE VESSEL IS FINISHED IT WILL SET SAIL IN THE BAY OF BENGAL.

A GROUP OF DAULATKHAN FISHERMEN POSE FOR A PHOTOGRAPH.

A YOUNG BOY AMONGST THE FISHING BOATS MOORED
JUST OUTSIDE OF DAULATKHAN, BANGLADESH.

THE BOX OFFICE
ATTENDANT FOR THE
SMALL CINEMA IN
DAULATKHAN. TO
PURCHASE YOUR TICKET
YOU BLINDLY PASS YOUR
MONEY IN THROUGH
THIS SMALL HOLE. THE
ATTENDANT COLLECTS IT
AND PUTS THE TICKET
IN YOUR HAND. THE
THEATRE ONLY SHOWS
THREE MOVIES AND THE
BUILDING ITSELF LOOKS
LIKE SOMETHING OUT
OF A HORROR FILM.

IN DAULATKHAN IT'S HARD NOT TO ATTRACT ATTENTION, ESPECIALLY WHEN YOU ARE THE ONLY CAUCASIAN SOME PEOPLE HAVE EVER SEEN FIRST-HAND. I'D SPOTTED THIS CLINT EASTWOOD LOOKALIKE EARLIER BUT WAS NOT ABLE TO GET A PHOTO OF HIM BY HIMSELF. WHY NOT JUST GO WITH IT AND PUT THE CROWD IN THE PICTURE TOO.

AN OLD FISHERMAN IN A
SMALL VILLAGE OUTSIDE
DAULATKHAN, BANGLADESH.

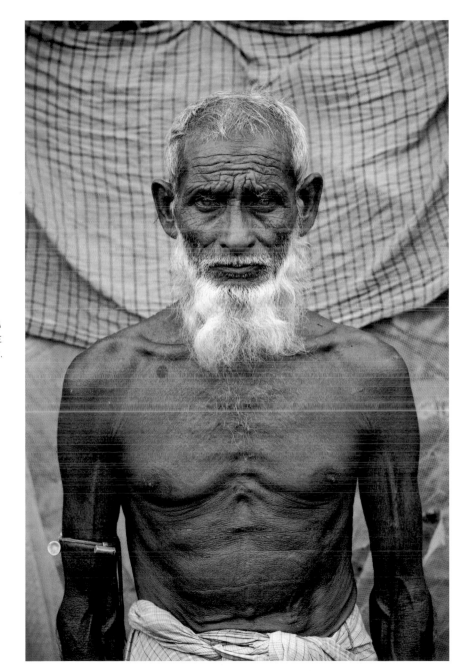

A BOY NAMED SOHEL CLIMBING
A TREE AFTER A SWIM IN ONE
OF THE IRRIGATION CANALS
NEAR DAULATKHAN.

AN ELDERLY MAN ENJOYING A WASH IN THE MEGHNA RIVER.

A YOUNG GIRL ALLOWS ME TO TAKE HER PORTRAIT AMONG THE
FISHING NETS ALONG THE BANKS OF THE MEGHNA.

A MEGHNA FISHERMAN TAKING A NAP WHILE HIS NETS ARE DRYING.

A YOUNG BOY SURROUNDED BY THE MEGHNA
RIVER IN SOUTHERN BANGLADESH.

A MAN SHOWING OFF HIS CATCH FROM A
MORNING OF FISHING ON THE MEGHNA.

A YOUNG BOY AND HIS FATHER BEFORE HEADING
OUT ON THE RIVER TO CATCH SOME FISH.

A YOUNG BOY POSES FOR ME
WHILE PLAYING FOOTBALL
IN THE MEGHNA MUD.

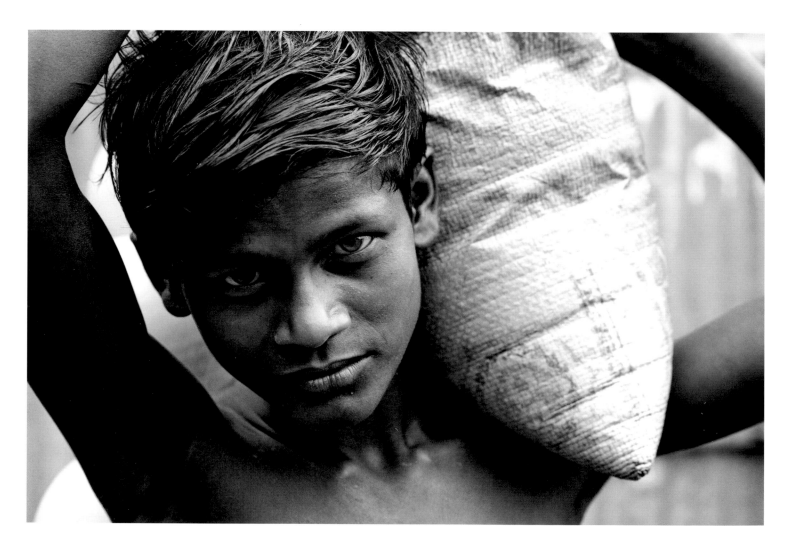

I SPOTTED THIS YOUNG BOY AS I WAS GOING FOR A WALK IN
A SMALL FISHING VILLAGE JUST OUTSIDE OF DAULATKHAN.
HIS EYES ARE WHAT ATTRACTED ME TO TAKE HIS PORTRAIT.

194

A GROUP OF BOYS POSE FOR A PHOTOGRAPH
AS I INTERRUPT THEIR FOOTBALL MATCH.

A GROUP OF BOYS DOING WHAT THEY DO BEST ... HAVING FUN.

A GROUP OF BOYS JOSTLING FOR CENTRE FRAME.

MEGHNA RIVER FISHERMEN WAITING FOR THEIR
NET TO DRIFT WITH THE CURRENT AND FILL
WITH FISH BEFORE HAULING IT IN BY HAND.

PORTRAIT OF
A BENGALI
FISHERMAN.

THIS YOUNG BOY I CAUGHT
TRYING TO STEAL MONEY FROM
MY WALLET. AFTER CALLING A
TRUCE WE BECAME REALLY GOOD
BUDDIES. HIS NAME IS SIRAJ.

ACKNOWLEDGEMENTS

First off, I would not have come this far in my photography personally and as a business without the love and continued support of my entire family. Thank you to Chris, Sandy, Adelaide, Briony, Luke, Natasha, Scott, Anna, Jesse, Stella and of course my mom and dad: Pam and Ron Fokkens. Thank you for always being there even when the genuine intentions behind all my ideas seemed a little crazy. Everyone's constant support has never gone unnoticed and I am your biggest fan.

To my closest friends both in Calgary and abroad, your love and words of encouragement I will never forget, and I thank you for always being there even when I was far away in another country.

I would also like to thank the amazing people I met overseas who welcomed me into their homes: Katia Verault, Mark Jordans and their son Sayam. Thank you for all the amazing soccer games in the front courtyard, your hospitality and your incredible outlook on life. I will never forget you. A huge shout-out to Salsa Nepal Dance Studios for your incredible thirst for dance and for letting me teach your enthusiastic students. Also thank you, Fanny Vandewiele, for your kindness and for allowing me to join you in Pashupatinath. Thanks as well to Ashok Bhandari, my Kathmandu guide. Your energy and enthusiasm for showing me Nepal has been and will always be unforgettable.

A massive thank you to Minhaj Chowdhury for all your help answering any questions I had and for just being a great friend. I will never forget all the good times we spent in Dhaka, and I look forward to when our paths cross in the near future.

A huge thank you to Xulhaz Mannan for your beautiful heart and generous hospitality and for giving me a bed to sleep on when I first arrived in Dhaka.

Thank you, Christy Sommers, for your knowledge, opinions and enthusiasm. I will miss our coffee dates and conversations about everything and anything.

Also thank you to Tanvir Hossain and Courtney Sato for being the best roommates ever and for the fun times we spent together.

I would like to thank everyone at RMB (Rocky Mountain Books), specifically publisher Don Gorman, art director Chyla Cardinal and especially editor Joe Wilderson. Thank you for believing in my work and for this incredible opportunity to share my stories and photographs.

I would also like to thank the photographic community for their continual support in my career. I am so lucky to be a colleague of such an amazing group of people and I cannot imagine a better community to be a part of.

Last but not least I would like to send my most sincere gratitude to every single one of the subjects I had the honour of photographing in Nepal and Bangladesh, including the random strangers and individuals who helped me find my way even when I couldn't read the bus numbers fast enough. I cannot put into words the amount of respect and appreciation I have for all of you. I thank you for the lessons you have taught me, the many cups of chai we shared, your beautiful smiles and for always trusting me.

ABOUT THE AUTHOR

Jeremy Fokkens is a Calgary-based professional portrait and documentary photographer who grew up in western Canada and initially trained as a classical dancer. It was while dancing overseas that he taught himself photography, and he now travels extensively to both developed and developing countries, inspiring viewers on a social and personal level while visually telling stories of people from all walks of life. Jeremy's work has been honoured by Nikon, TEDx Dhaka and Invisible Photographer Asia, and he has been a finalist for the Black & White Spider Awards and for International Travel Photographer of the Year in both 2011 and 2012. His photographs have been featured in group and solo exhibitions throughout Canada and the United States. To see more of Jeremy's work, please visit www.jeremyfokkens.com.

Rocky Mountain Books
www.rmbooks.com

Library and Archives Canada Cataloguing in Publication

Fokkens, Jeremy, author, photographer
The human connection : photographs and stories from Bangladesh and Nepal / Jeremy Fokkens.

Issued in print and electronic formats.
ISBN 978-1-77160-057-6 (bound).—ISBN 978-1-77160-058-3 (html).—
ISBN 978-1-77160-059-0 (pdf)

1. Fokkens, Jeremy—Travel—Bangladesh. 2. Fokkens, Jeremy—Travel—Nepal. 3. Bangladesh—Description and travel. 4. Nepal—Description and travel. 5. Bangladesh—Social life and customs—21st century—Pictorial works. 6. Nepal—Social life and customs—21st century—Pictorial works. I. Title.

DS393.5.F64 2014   915.49204'5   C2014-904036-9
C2014-904037-7W

Printed in China

Rocky Mountain Books acknowledges the financial support for its publishing program from the Government of Canada through the Canada Book Fund (CBF) and the Canada Council for the Arts, and from the province of British Columbia through the British Columbia Arts Council and the Book Publishing Tax Credit.

 Canadian Heritage   Patrimoine canadien   Canada Council for the Arts   Conseil des Arts du Canada

 BRITISH COLUMBIA ARTS COUNCIL
Supported by the Province of British Columbia

This book was produced using FSC®-certified, acid-free paper, processed chlorine free and printed with soya-based inks.